Books by Keith Dahlberg

Edwin T. Dahlberg, Pastor, Peacemaker, Prophet
(biography)

Flame Tree, A Novel of Modern Burma

Bridge Ahead, A Medical Memoir

Access to Medical Care

ACCESS TO MEDICAL CARE

COMMON SENSE FOR DOCTORS, PATIENTS, and the PUBLIC

KEITH DAHLBERG, MD

iUniverse, Inc.
New York   Bloomington

ACCESS TO MEDICAL CARE
COMMON SENSE FOR DOCTORS,
PATIENTS, and the PUBLIC

iUniverse books may be ordered through booksellers or by contacting:

iUniverse
1663 Liberty Drive
Bloomington, IN 47403
www.iuniverse.com
1-800-Authors (1-800-288-4677)

Because of the dynamic nature of the Internet, any Web addresses or links contained in this book may have changed since publication and may no longer be valid. The views expressed in this work are solely those of the author and do not necessarily reflect the views of the publisher, and the publisher hereby disclaims any responsibility for them.

ISBN: 978-1-4401-7452-0 (pbk)
ISBN: 978-1-4401-7451-3 (ebook)

Printed in the United States of America

iUniverse rev. date: 9/28/09

TABLE OF CONTENTS

PREFACE

Most Americans agree that the cost of medical care is growing out of control, but we disagree on a solution. Some say, "Keep government out of it. Let private enterprise fix the problem, like it has always done." Others reply, "Everyone needs access to medical care, but it is being priced beyond our ability to pay for it." Private enterprise has not fixed it, so far, and the cost is still rising. It's not going to get better by itself.

The President and Congress are trying to respond to the need, with some progress, but no consensus yet at the time of this writing.

President Obama has (in my opinion) chosen some practical goals:

1) Affordable medical insurance for all Americans
2) Emphasize preventive care
3) Electronic records
4) Lowering over-all cost while maintaining quality of care, by addressing cost overruns, fraud, education methods that don't work, and getting the waste out of entitlement programs (Medicare, Medicaid, VA, etc.)

Some people object to the cost, some others doubt that government bureaucrats can keep anything simple; still others object because their beliefs oppose drastic change to the status quo. But the continuing growth of the present medical delivery system will very soon make that status quo unreachable even for a nation as rich as the United States.

The purpose should not be to construct a large new expensive system. The goal is to *lower* the overall cost while improving the care. That turns out to be a complicated job.

Personal Disclaimer and Credentials: The purpose of this small book is not to promote a political viewpoint, but to suggest some practical ways to help reach the goal of access to medical care for all.

My suggestions are based on a half century in medical practice, in America and abroad, plus opinions offered by neighbors, patients, and professional colleagues along the way. No one's experience is complete, and I welcome any reasoned counter-arguments to what I have to say.

I entered the medical system in 1948, as a hospital orderly and ambulance rider. I completed college in 1950 (pre-med, BA in chemistry, at Syracuse University.) I earned my MD in 1954 from SUNY's Upstate Medical University at Syracuse. My internship and residency training was at Denver's Presbyterian Hospital (one year each in general internship, obstetrics, and surgery.)

I joined an American overseas organization and spent the next ten years practicing tropical medicine and general surgery, opening and managing a hospital, first in Burma and then another in Thailand. I was a doctor on salary, working amid a national socialized medicine environment.

Beginning in 1967, I entered private medical practice in an Idaho mining town, first in a group, later solo, plus another four-year term in Thailand. In 1994 I retired from full-time work at age sixty-five. I spent the next ten years in part time work ("locum tenens"), filling temporary vacancies in hospitals, ERs, and doctors' offices, ranging over much of the United States, and three foreign nations.

I have a wife and three daughters, all RNs, active in various fields of hospital management[1], and a son in professional money management. Each of them makes comments I find worth listening to.

Much of medical care delivery depends on common sense and perhaps a heightened sense of responsibility in doctors, patients, insurance companies, and government; sometimes in all four.

Acknowledgments: Patients and illustrative anecdotes are kept anonymous out of respect for their privacy. They are not limited to any one locality.

I am grateful for editorial and informative comments from family and colleagues, and to technical support from iUniverse of Bloomington, Indiana, and ALS computers of Wallace, Idaho for   assistance in preparing this book.

Keith Dahlberg

CHAPTER ONE:

DEALING WITH OUR FEAR OF THE FUTURE

"How can we possibly pay for medical care for forty-five million more people without insurance?" The answer is, you are already paying for it, and at more than three times the amount it should cost.

These uninsured are not millions of newcomers to America. They are already here, in the system, our fellow citizens with low-paying jobs or no jobs at all. Doctors who are willing to accept some non-paying patients are already seeing them every day of the week.

Every time any of those forty-five million gets sick or injured but can't get in to see a doctor, they go to the hospital emergency room, the only place that by law must accept and examine them, and give them emergency care. Usually the ER doctor on duty has not seen that person before and must do a reasonably complete exam plus lab tests to know what's going on. The charge for an emergency room visit, as many readers know all too well, averages over $1,000, compared with an average for an office visit or urgent care center of $150 [2].

Every time an uninsured patient, who can't pay for his care out of pocket, gets medical care at an emergency room, you—and all of us—are paying the cost of his care out of our present taxes or the increased rate a hospital must charge to make up for what they can't collect from the non-payer. These 45,000,000 are already in the system, and we are already paying their costs. It makes sense to get their colds and minor injuries *out* of the ER and into the doctor's office, at less than one-fifth the cost we are paying now. That alone would save about half the alleged trillion dollars of new insurance premiums.

In addition, instead of getting medical care after his condition has reached crisis proportions, the newly insured can get preventive care or early care, reducing chances of his needing hospitalization later on (where the cost of care is even higher than the ER.)

It's true that when the presently uninsured get insurance, they will use doctors more often, but the increased need for doctors will not be like all the newly insured are just getting off the boat and entering the country. They are already here. And when doctors know that insurance will pay something for every patient, you will see more men and women entering medicine as a career, and increasing the number of doctors available. There are ways that America could use its doctors more effectively, and we'll take a look at that in chapter fourteen, Watchdogs and Government.

American emergency care is very good, but very expensive. Driving Interstate 90 one day, over in Montana, I came upon a bad highway accident. A van pulling a light trailer had crashed into the Jersey barrier and was now on fire. The driver had pulled each of his three children unharmed out of the car, but suffered severe burns himself, while trying to save his wife until the flames forced him away. The State Patrol had arrived, the fire department was on its way. Not only was the car ablaze, but the heat began exploding rifle cartridges in the trailer, just about the time I was offerng my services as an ER physician to the trooper in charge. He and I took shelter from the bullets, crouching behind the concrete barrier, while he asked me to look at the driver who was now lying on a blanket some distance away.

The driver was a man in his thirties; I estimated he had a 60 to 80% body burn, and he appeared to be in shock. There was nothing we could do for him except assure him the helicopter was on its way, and keep him sheltered from the hot sun. Presently the 'copter arrived, with a trauma team who stabilized him as best they could. They took him to the regional hospital, to be further stabilized and forwarded by air to the burn center at Salt Lake City. The trooper arranged for the three children to be driven to the local hospital, where social services would take charge. Their mother had died in the fire.

This is what emergency work is intended to be—a badly injured person reaching specialized care quickly. In such a crisis, the question of payment in advance never comes up. Professionals and neighbors do what they can, never mind the cost.

But forty-five million people who have no family doctor, and who usually see a different care giver, with a charge for a new patient visit almost every time they are ill? That is a much bigger problem, and requires a much more organized solution than it has now.

Are They Gonna Make Grandma Die?!   Such talk is utter nonsense. More than that, it's deliberate mis-information, spread by those who would fan flames of rage, and break up town meetings intended to explain medical care proposals. There are many who have valid questions and doubts about parts of the Health Care proposals, but no one proposes killing off the old folks or leaving them untreated and alone to die.

I have observed many cheerful patients in their eighties and nineties who live active lives at home with mental function intact. I have also seen others lying unresponsive or barely conscious in bed for months. There are still others whose body is kept artificially alive on respirators, tube-feedings, and wires, with no real hope of ever recovering natural brain or body functions.

That's why doctors and hospitals encourage people to decide for themselves, while they are still well and can communicate their wishes, to make a "living will" that instructs how far to go in maintaining life. That's a choice each person should make, and update from time to time. I update my own every year or two, and make sure my doctor and any hospital I go to has a copy.

Each person has the right to choose for himself. That's what the lawmakers are trying to guarantee. All of us will be old some day.

What about the loss of jobs in the medical insurance business, if the uninsured get "public option" insurance? Let's run that one by again. These uninsured people are, by definition, not insured. These are the millions of people the insurance companies considered not worth the risk of insuring. It's the other 260 million Americans the present number of insurance salesmen and their companies service. So who's job is getting lost?

But what if the government "public option" or "co-op option insurance" undersells the private companies? Won't about nineteen million already-insured people switch over?

Not if it's handled sensibly. I don't know where that 19 million figure came from, or what Congress will finally decide, but I would expect high income and middle income people would not be eligible for a public plan. And if the private companies suddenly discover that some who have a pre-existing illness, or who work for a small business are worth insuring after all, fine! If some of those companies feel that big bonuses for their executives are a better way of using their profits, that's up to them. According to the rules of free enterprise, such decisions can make them or break them.

I sincerely hope the Government doesn't want to take over the whole insurance industry. The object of getting medical insurance for everyone is not to gain control over their lives, but to have a healthy population where most people are able to work, able to educate their children, pay their share of taxes, pay for the things they want to buy, and hope to lay something aside for retirement. Actually, that plan works in many independent and prosperous nations.

But it's more complicated than just getting everybody insurance. Let's take a look at some of the other pieces in the puzzle.

Chapter Two:

What Makes Medical Costs Rise So Fast?

The first car my wife and I ever bought back in 1954 cost a hundred dollars. It was a 1937 Plymouth sedan in need of paint, with no add-ons that I can remember, except a heater. No clock, no automatic shift or overdrive gear; microchip controls did not yet exist, but it got us where we needed to go.

Our car in the 1960's, a VW microbus, cost around $2,000 new. It had seat belts, a radio, space for four kids, and better gas mileage. And nowadays, we're lucky to get a low-end Honda with cruise control, airbags, and automatic locks for about $17,000. As cars add equipment and safety features, they cost more to build, including wage increases and benefits for people on the assembly line.

But there comes a point where further improvements make the car cost too much. As things stand, my car gets me where I'm going in relative comfort and good gas mileage. I can live with the dent in the fender and the road noise. I don't need an upgrade to a fancier car to tell me who I am.

Same with medical care. In the 1950's, doctors could diagnose and cure pneumonia with a chest X-ray, blood count, sputum exam, some penicillin, and a bottle of cough syrup. Older people remember that era, and call it the good old days.

In those same "good old days", people with leukemia or a heart attack usually died.

Nowadays, most leukemia can be suppressed, and in most heart attacks the blocked coronary arteries can be restored to function, saving the patient's life. But all the machines, new tests, and highly trained technicians to make that possible send the cost way up. A CT-scan machine costs a hospital a million dollars, and an MRI scanner even more. We reach a point where not every hospital can afford an MRI machine or a coronary care unit, nor the technically trained staff to run them, even though the market may be there.

When I was a hospital orderly in the 1940's, hospitals needed a staff (nurses, clerks, janitors included) of one worker for each patient. When I ended my medical practice a few years ago, the ratio was 3 staff members for every patient. Now I am told the ratio is 4 to 1 and still rising. There are respiratory care techs, quality control people to prevent errors, more insurance clerks, computer techs to run the systems; all need to be paid for what they do. Nurses who used to carry bedpans and give out sleeping pills now have to interpret complicated heart monitors, blood gases and oxygen saturation. Not to mention carefully assessing the effects of multiple simultaneous IV medication drips as matters of routine.

Highly trained nurses and doctors kept me alive after my seven-hour heart surgery three years ago. I recall, in the mental fog while coming out of anesthesia, overhearing one nurse say to another at my bedside, "Now give him one unit of insulin in the IV."

"I'm not diabetic," I remember objecting.

"We know," one said, "but with the stress this kind of surgery puts on your body, the survival rate is much better if we keep your blood sugar exactly under control for the first couple of days."

I hadn't known that, but to the nurses in the critical care unit, such knowledge is routine. I consider such competence worth the higher earnings these nurses make now. But most local hospitals can't support all that technology; many people have to travel hundreds of miles to find such care.

Many medical costs rarely existed fifty years ago. Doctors now have educational loans that may take them ten or twenty years to pay off, they pay high malpractice insurance premiums to cover the lawsuit they will get sometime in their career, no matter how careful they are. And any doctor worth his salt continues updating his skills throughout his career, with the added expense and time of attending conferences taken out from the work he gets paid for. Some of the increasing costs of medical care are unavoidable. Many of those new specialty technicians have families to support, and none of them can work for free.

But one thing is for sure: America is not going to get 2010-type care for 1950-type prices.

Chapter Three:

The Costliest Medical Tool

Dr. Atul Gawande is a Boston surgeon who, in his widely acclaimed article, *The Cost Conundrum* (The New Yorker, June 1, 2009), investigates the difference in cost of medical care in two similar Texas cities, McAllen and El Paso.

Both of these cities have a metropolitan area roughly the same in population, size and composition. Both are near the Mexican border, both have well-equipped hospitals and competent doctors concerned with giving good treatment to their patients. (I won't go into detailed statistics here; you can find the article online or at any city library.) The remarkable thing that Dr. Gawande found was that in McAllen, Medicare is spending $15,000 per enrollee per year, about twice the national average; and in El Paso only $7,504 per enrollee, just half as much. Fourteen years before, the two rates were each about equal to the national average, and El Paso's still is.

The main difference in Medicare charges had little to do with equipment or available services, which were about equally good and up-to-date in both cities, and had little to do with lawsuits (much fewer in Texas, which caps the amount of non-medical damages.) Basically, Medicare was paying more because many of the doctors in McAllen were ordering more tests, more operations, more specialist consults, more diagnostic procedures, as shown by the insurance records. Dr.

Gawande observes that the Mayo Clinic in Minnesota can, and does, provide much more elaborate care, at less than half the overall price per capita, compared with McAllen.

The most costly instrument that doctors use, in terms of its effect, Dr. Gawande offers, is the pen with which doctors order prescriptions, lab tests, and procedures. (The pen costs less than a dollar, of course. It's the doctor who uses the pen who controls the costs.) He goes into lengthy discussion of the reasons some doctors order more tests, more treatment, more specialists' consultations than others do, but the end result is clear. Doctors' orders are written by doctors. Not hospital administrators, not insurance clerks, not government bureaucrats. Though the rules established by any of the latter three groups may influence what doctors order, none of them are trained or equipped to judge what's best for the individual patient's case. That's the doctor's job. Many doctors are not paying much attention to the price a patient (or his insurance) pays, but they should. By doctors giving more thought to the price of the things they order, the cost of medical care—be it covered by private insurance, government program, or patient's own pocket—the cost of medical care in America could be reduced by several hundred billion dollars per year with little or no harmful effect on quality of care. That's if doctors pay attention to the price and actual need of what they are ordering. Think cost-effectiveness.

I see no point in duplicating the anecdotes from the New Yorker article; I can supply plenty of my own, as can most other doctors. Here are a few of mine:

Chapter Four:

The Medicine She Never Took

"My doctor gave me a new medicine for my stomach pain," a friend answered when I expressed hope that she was feeling well. "It works fine, but I can't take it."

"I'm sorry to hear that," I said. "Too many side effects?"

"No, the samples he gave me helped a lot. But when I took his prescription to the pharmacy, a month's supply was four hundred dollars. That's almost half my Social Security check! How am I going to pay my utility bills and buy my groceries? So I'll just keep on with the antacids."

"Did you tell your doctor you couldn't pay that kind of price?"

"I phoned him, and he said he had no idea it was that high."

"Did you ask him about any of the over-the-counter medicines? Some of them are about one-tenth that price, or less."

"No, I didn't know anything about that. He had his make me an appointment for two weeks from now for follow-up. But I never had the prescription filled when I found out the cost."

If you think that's an isolated example, another patient had had at least six back surgeries over the years (laminectomy) and no surgeon would now touch his scarred back. His local doctor was ftrying to manage the pain with various pills and patches, some of which eased his steady pain, but not the "lightning spasms" that struck when he moved wrong. Additonally, over the years, he had developed unacceptable reactions to some of the medicines, and the doctor was trying a new one. His medical insurance refused to pay for it. The doctor's office clerk said she would try and straighten the matter out, and would call him back. She never did, nor even to let him know the problem. He finally called his pharmacist to see if he could afford to pay for it himself, and found to his horror that a month's supply was $525.00, half his entire monthy income. Presumably, the doctor's clerk could have found that out, but if she did, she never let him know.

These illustrate a basic flaw in the American way of marketing medicines. The manufacturers have well-paid "detail persons" who make regular calls at each and every doctor's office to inform him/her about their company's latest and most advanced product. They sometimes used to appear around noon, with enough pizza for the whole office staff. Friendly people, well trained and informed in their field, they are a principle source of information for busy doctors who don't spend as much time as they might with medical journals and Internet search. The pharmaceutical rep has free samples to leave with the doctor, along with note pads or pens bearing the product's name.

Sometimes they really do have valuable updates for the doctor, but they rarely mention the price of their product, or that the older remedies still work as well as they always did. And the doctor will try the samples on his patients because (a) he doesn't want them to buy a whole month's supply of any medicine unless he knows it works for them, and/or (b) he may want to help a patient he knows is having difficulty affording care.

Most doctors don't keep up with the present-day price of what they prescribe. But they could. Every doctor gets an annual free update of Physician's Desk Reference listing all prescription medicines with their uses, side effects, and precautions (about 4,000+ pages—old copies make good doorstops), and a supplement with all the non-prescription medicines is available as well. Plus an annual update of Redbook (not the women's fashions one, but current drug retail prices) with the option of subscribing to monthly updates.

So - **here's what a patient can do**. Don't be afraid to ask what a new prescription will cost, and if necessary, ask if there is a less expensive generic that will be adequate. Sometimes there will be, sometimes not.

And **Doctors, here's what you can do.** Be aware that the latest drug is pushed by the drug rep because that's what he/she is hired to do. It's good to keep that product in mind, but ask yourself, "Is this what this patient sitting here in front of me really needs, or will an older, less expensive drug be effective?" And stay away from reps who want to buy you meals or pay for a vacation trip. Your patients have to pay for that in the cost of their medicine.

And all you readers in the general public, pressure your reps in Congress to reasonably regulate the charges for medicines. Why should a drug that has been on the market eleven years now cost fifteen dollars per pill when the company was raking in high profits at the original price of ten dollars per pill? Why should an injection aimed at mass use be selling for thirty-five dollars, when it originally wholesaled forty years ago at one dollar? Or why should a drug, manufactured in USA, sell for less in Canada or Europe than it does here where it was made?

Even in a free market economy, the customer should get as much consideration as the company's stock holders get.

Chapter Five:

Some Other Medical Costs under Doctors' Control have Less Acceptable Reasons to Exist.

Unbundling the charges: This means charging separately for each part of a service: for example, when a doctor charges for the surgery, and then adds on extra charges for the local anesthetic, the sutures, dressings, the office visit and the return visit for suture removal. Fortunately, most insurance companies and government agencies now require the doctor to "bundle" all the surgery-related items into a single charge.

Raising the charge to compensate for an insurance carrier paying only a part of the total. As an example, a patient I know was charged seven thousand dollars for a one-hour office procedure. Yes, the materials and electronic device the doctor used were pricey, but not that much. I checked the price online, and the machine he was using cost about $35,000, but he could use it over and over. Even one such procedure per month, billed at seven thousand would bring in about eighty-four thousand dollars each year, if everyone paid the charge. When I asked on the patient's behalf, the doctor's office explained that the insurance carrier paid only about half of whatever amount he charged. I asked what if the patient has no insurance? "That would be taken into consideration." Meaning?

Professional courtesy to doctors and their families. The 2,500-year-old Hippocratic Oath tells doctors they shouldn't charge a fee when treating their teachers or other doctors. But times change. Nowadays I believe the average doctor, above almost everyone else, can afford medical insurance for himself and his family, and has little reason not to pay his fair share of medical costs. We doctors might think more about how much to charge our patients if we were to personally experience the effect of present-day medical bills.

Building new facilities for personal profit rather than community need: You will sometimes see special suites or other construction added on to hospitals, but owned by a group of private doctors. To the extent that such a place supplies functions not available elsewhere in the area, they can be good. To the extent that they duplicate services already in the community, they can add to patients' cost and risk.

For instance, a "cardiac cath" (a study of patient's coronary arteries supplying the heart muscle) involves specialized training and care. If the procedure shows the need for a "stent" to keep the artery open, it requires more of a safety net, in a hospital with a critical care ward backup. The stent usually can be inserted at the time of the first cath, but if the specialist's work place is in a separate building, he may choose to do all his caths at his own cath lab, and send only those patients who turn out to need a stent over to the hospital. The stent patient thus undergoes two separate procedures, and two anesthetics, when both the diagnosis and treatment could have been done as a single procedure in the hospital, with less risk and less total cost.

Chapter Six:

Making access to a doctor easier

"Getting there is half the fun." Yeah, right. Your six-year-old wakes up this morning with a really sore throat, a cough and a fever. Or maybe she has an earache. Or perhaps you've found a lump in your breast. Your doctor's telephone receptionist gives you the run-around, "Our next open appointment is in six days. If you're really concerned, go to the hospital emergency room . . .would you like their number?"

No, thanks, you already have their number. A doctor who has never seen you before, and likely will not be on call the next time either, will put an automatic thermometer in your kid's ear, glance down her throat, and give you a prescription for a cough syrup you've already tried at home. See your doctor in three days if there's no improvement. Your doctor's already-full schedule isn't the ER doc's problem. You'll get a bill for several days worth of your wages, and are no better off than before you came in. The ER doc is reasonably sure your child will be better soon, but he fails to convince you.

This really doesn't need to happen. You shouldn't have to use the expensive ER for an urgent, but non-emergency problem just because no doctor's office has any time open.

Doctors who allow the front desk to fill their appointment schedule completely full ahead of time are not thinking things through. Common sense will tell any primary care doctor that many people's sickness appears without warning and they need help today, not next week or next month. And people who only need a follow-up visit usually don't care if their next appointment is seven days or seventeen days from now, as long as they know they have one.

During my partnership days, my partners' habits drove me crazy. They all booked all their time in advance; one doc overbooked two extra people for each hour, "because someone might not show up." Our large waiting room was often full of irate patients, waiting as much as three hours after their appointment time. My partners were good doctors, but were clueless about office management, as long as the office looked busy. "The patients can always get in; they just have to wait a while if we're busy."

I decided, because of several management reasons, that I could run an office better by leaving the partnership and going solo, and I did.

Here is what works: The doctor sits down with his staff and they decide how much the average routine visit takes of the doctor's time. Not how long he'd like it to take, but how long it really does take, according to the people who work with him. Say, for example, that on average he can handle four visits per hour. More complex problems—a new patient, or a new pregnancy— might take 30 minutes or an hour, and so would have one or more extra time slots assigned. In my own practice, I could usually handle repeat office visits in 15 minutes. After saving some time for hospital rounds, record-keeping, minor surgery, etc., I usually had around six hours per day for patients' office visits.

I told my receptionist she could fill two 15-minute slots for each hour ahead of the day. A third one each hour could be filled from the phone calls of people who wanted to get in that day for something they thought urgent. The fourth slot each hour was saved for walk-ins. People rarely had to wait more than 10 minutes beyond their appointment time, unless I had emergency surgery, or a baby delivery in progress.

Was it a problem to have an occasional empty appointment slot? Not for me it wasn't. I used the time to return phone calls, sign or dictate letters, catch up on my medical journals, order supplies, or enjoy a cup of coffee at my desk. My patients were more relaxed, and so was I, not having to keep pace with an always-over-full schedule. I found that it's not always necessary to bring someone in each month, just for a blood pressure check or a blood sugar, once their condition was stabilized.

Not every patient who only had a question needed an appointment; sometimes the question could be handled by phone. My receptionist brought the patient's medical record to my desk along with the call-back number. She only called me out of a patient's examining room if she judged the call truly urgent, or if another doctor was calling about a patient, but I tried to answer the less urgent calls as soon as possible.

This system of scheduling even gave me time to see some people who hadn't been able to get in to see their own doctor. Many had a problem that could be dealt with in a single visit, after which they could go back to the other doctor again. A cut finger, or a rash, or sawdust in an eye, didn't always require a full history and physical exam to treat.

So - **Doctors, rethink your appointment scheduling.** Packing your schedule full ahead of time causes tension, always trying to keep up, and it makes your waiting patients fidgety, even miserable if they are feeling pain or are otherwise ill. You'll also be more efficient if you get in the habit of starting work on time, and limiting the length of your coffee break. (Read that newspaper at home.)

Receptionist, if the doctor is behind schedule (and hey, it can happen) let the patients know. If the doc is way behind, offer to reschedule them. If he's *avoidably* behind very often, let *him* know.

For those doctors who are overwhelmed by the number of patients they must see, I don't mean to imply that I don't know what patient overload is like. In Asian hospitals where I was the only doctor, there were times when a major road accident brought in eight or ten critically injured people, with no doctor backup to call on. Or there were thirty patients in line outside the door. Or surgery that kept me up all night. I have occasionally worked 24 hours on and 24 off in emergency rooms, under ACLS and ATLS[3] standards.

In some cases, adding a nurse-practitioner or physician's assistant to the office is an option. In other cases, better pay and benefits for the office staff will help keep efficient workers instead of orienting new ones all the time. In other cases, work on tort reform, or reduction of paperwork at the state, rather than federal level may actually prove faster, once the first few states have shown what works.

The basic problem is how to motivate more new doctors to choose primary care instead of specialties. This gets into issues of student clinical clerkships in disadvantaged neighborhoods, or in underdeveloped countries; ways to catch the attention of doctors in their student or residency years. These are issues beyond the scope of this brief book, but which are badly in need of attention.

Chapter Seven:

Payment up front, and the uninsured

Somehow, in America, medical insurance became connected to who you work for. It's not that way in every country, but it's one way of getting medical bills paid, if someone in your family has a well-paying job.

Not everyone does. Some don't have a family. Some work for minimum wage. Some can find only part-time work, and it doesn' t usually include medical benefits. Some are sick or disabled, and can't work. For some of you, what the doctor charges for a first office visit (which some doctors define as the first visit for a new illness, even if you've been coming there for years) is more than you earn in half a week or more. So you wait and hope it'll get better by itself. And if it doesn't, the medical cost will go even higher.

Maybe some day our United States will take the same path that so many other nations have travelled and have a system which doesn't leave millions of people with no way to pay for illness. I've worked under such systems (in Thailand and in Myanmar) and they had problems of their own. In Thailand, everyone could come to the hospital, and many of the doctors were well-trained, but the hospital shelves were sometimes empty of medicines or other supplies, and then the patient's family might have to go buy his medicine outside somewhere.

And not all services were available immediately. There may be a waiting list. That's a trade-off some nations must make for having at least basic care available to every one.[4]

In northern Idaho, I live close enough to the Canadian border to have had occasional Canadians as patients (now residing in US, or tourists.) The majority of them say they are quite pleased with the Canadian system, where their government pays, even though some treatments involve delay.

Like everyone else, American doctors, nurses, techs, hospital janitors, and clerks all make their living from the work they do; they can't work for free all the time. Ordinarily, the doctor's office rent, payroll, cost of office equipment, etc. are also paid from the fees he collects. So it's reasonable to expect that his monthly work income has to be greater than, say, that of a fireman or a foundry foreman, even though those jobs may also involve danger, special training, and irregular hours.

The doctor's job does not give him license to charge whatever the market will bear, of course. There are about 650,000 full-time physicians treating patients nowadays in the USA. (Most of the rest have salaried jobs in teaching or research.) The difference between an average take-home pay (before taxes) of $100,000 and $200,000 per doctor per year adds $65 billion to the annual health costs of the country. According to one medical recruiting firm[5], the average income of family physicians, (one of the lower-paying medical specialties) is $173,000 per year. Specialists often get two or three times that.

I won't presume to set income limits for my medical colleagues, but here is my own experience: In the last four full years of my full-time office practice (Jan. 1989 to Dec.1992) my own practice income averaged $124,000 per year, of which 64,000 went for expenses (payroll, insurance, building maintenance, supplies, etc.) leaving a take-home pay averaging

$60,000 per year before taxes. I suppose the intervening years of inflation would bring that figure closer to the $173,000 family practice doctors average nowadays.

Be that as it may, I am disturbed by the well-documented facts of Dr. Gawande's survey (discussed earlier), where medical costs per patient were twice as much in one city as they were in a nearby city, with little or no difference in the results of care. Most doctors do their best to take good care of their patients, but some overtreat, overtest, and overprescribe. Possibly, they want to be as sure as they can to find the cause of illness and completely correct it. It may be they are trying to avoid malpractice suits from over-zealous lawyers. Or it may be gradual ethics-creep, where some doctors come to believe the world owes them a better living than those around them, and deliberately pursue a high income as their main goal, at their patients' expense.

The doctor's primary purpose is to serve the people who come to him, not to feed off them. No amount of country club memberships, luxury homes, cars, or clothing, no fattening of the bank account can compensate for neglect of the healer's responsibility to heal.

The sick and injured come first. Then your staff, then you. Not the other way around.

But doctors also have a valid complaint when, in an effort to economize in hard economic times, government or insurance companies cut payments and still expect the same work output. On the other hand, the payers have a solid counter-complaint when they point out how doctors' fees are rising faster than the cost of living. The solution? Several are possible:

1.) **Doctors can remedy the "pay-up-front" barrier themselves,** individually, taking the initiative out of the hands of the third-party payers. Many doctors already are doing this. I found a way for more of my patients to afford care; it's not so much the old or permanently disabled that are stymied by pay-up-front—they at least have someone to make partial payment for them. It's the low-income uninsured that have the biggest problem. In my last several years of office practice, I put a pre-printed note in every patient's first bill, telling them that if they are living on a small fixed income, or are out of work, they could reduce my charges, no explanation necessary. (I suggested 25% reduction, but left the amount of reduction up to them. It didn't apply to any portion paid by a third party.)

Other doctors have different ways of expressing it. It worked pretty well for me, and certainly helped the doctor-patient relationship. Maybe 10% of my patients ever used the offer at all, and only a very few tried to game the system.

And it didn't affect my income to any great degree. Medical economists have told me that most doctors' collection ratio (the total of all his fees that actually get paid) is around 90%. Mine was 87% when I figured up the last few years of my office practice. I lived on that quite well, even while accepting Medicare, Medicaid, and people with no insurance at all. Some patients needed a tactful reminder if they totally skipped more than two monthly payments, but I never had to take anyone to court.

2.) **A community low income clinic** staffed with volunteers is a partial solution. Even if it only meets once a week, and has few resources, the doctor there can at least answer questions, give routine exams, and refill prescriptions for medicines the patient has been taking for a long time—thyroid, blood pressure pills, etc. Locally here, the L.I.Clinic dispenses free sample meds when available, or gives vouchers for meds to take to one of several pharmacists (who bill the clinic at a reduced rate.) The doctor also applies directly to some pharmaceutical companies for free meds for certain patients requiring expensive medicines not available as generics.

Patients in our local clinic go through a financial check, and must be without insurance, and with an income below 200% of poverty level. Our local clinic now meets only twice a month because of a shortage of doctors. And, of course, patients sometimes really need to be in the hospital emergency room. The clinic gives the hospital a heads-up when one of their patients needs ER or hospital care, which is not very often. Such clinics are a part of many city and county public health networks, and can usually be found in the local phone directory, or online.

3.) **Doctors working on salary** are not rare. I did it, my first fifteen years after residency. Everyone in the organization got the same pay, adjusted for family size and for cost of living in the country where we worked. An outside agency determined country CLA. When everyone gets the same pay without regard to seniority or skills, the workplace can be much more pleasant. And even with long lines of patients; we saw many rare diseases, and had satisfaction in being able to help them.

I understand that some American medical clinics have their doctors on salary, the Mayo Clinic among them. The primary care doctor can call on any specialist among his colleagues for what we used to call "curbside consults", informal discussions among several doctors, who have no incentive to repeat laboratory tests, because they all use the same lab. It's no coincidence that such efficiency not only provides the best of care, but does it at a lower cost than the national average.

Chapter Eight:

Communicating With Your Doctor

Just so you won't think doctors as patients fare better than other people, let me tell you about my recent few days trying to find out "how my test came out".

After having major chest surgery, I learned that two of my relatives had the same problem I had had. I asked my doctor what the chances were of a hereditary defect in my aorta, the body's main artery, for myself and my relatives. He scheduled me for an ultrasound. "I'll be out of town next week," he said, "but one of my partners can give you the report."

So I went to the hospital; the ultrasound took about ten minutes. I admired the new ultrasound machine, asked the tech about it, and how my aorta looked. "I didn't see anything abnormal," she said. "The machine measured your aorta's width in the abdomen as 1.7 centimeters, but your doctor will talk to you about it," she said. The pictures are all sent electronically to a regional hospital 40 miles away to be read and reported.

Sunday morning, I got a worried call from the physician's assistant covering the weekend. "Hey, Doc, the radiologist reports you have an aneurysm in your abdomen. Nothing to worry about yet, but you should see your doctor when he gets back."

"Okay. What does it measure?"

"2.4 centimeters," [one inch; bigger than it should be, down in the abdomen.]

"The tech told me 1.7"

"Maybe she measured wrong."

"The new machine measures it automatically and prints a readout, doesn't it?" I said.

"Well, talk to your doctor about it next week."

Next day, the phone rang. "Please hold for Dr. G."

I waited while the phone told me, "this call may be monitored for quality assurance." And waited some more. Finally, "This is Dr. G." (one of the radiologists over in the city.)

"I believe you are calling me," I said.

"Oh, about your aneurysm. Nothing to really worry about; it's shrunk from 5.4 to 2.4 cm."

"No. The 5.4 centimeter one is the one they repaired last year."

"Aren't we talking about your ascending aorta?"

"No, that's been replaced with a graft. My ultrasound last week is of my abdomen."

"Well, that's 2.4 cm."

"How do we know it's my film? When the tech read the machine it said 1.7"

"The report has your name on it."

"Does the actual picture have my name on it? Maybe someone got two pictures mixed."

"You'd better talk to your doctor about it. He'll be back next week."

Eventually, my own doctor assured me my abdominal aorta was okay. But I never did find out why some reports said it was half-again as big as other reports said. What kind of precision is that?

Is there a point to all this? Sure. Don't be afraid to ask questions if you don't understand. If you hear two different things, find out why. Sometimes reports are mixed up, or the original tests are. Don't be a pest about it; play it cool, but politely express your wish to have the difference explained.

It gets even more frustrating for patients who aren't doctors.

Chapter Nine:

More on Communication

ER clerks and doctor's office nurses can sometimes frustrate patients as much as doctors can. A friend recalls going to the hospital in labor with her third child. She had a history of fast labors, and she arrived at the hospital with what she called "one continuous contraction."

"I need to go to the delivery room," she told the clerk.

"Well, first we need to get your name, address, and name of your insurance." The clerk was proceeding by rote, pen poised over clipboard.

"I need to go to the delivery room!" gasped her patient.

"Everyone is in a meeting just now," soothed the clerk. "Now, your name?"

"HERE COMES THE BABY!" That finally got the clerk's attention.

Fast forward fifty years: the same friend has been referred to a gastroenterologist by her family doctor. A nurse practitioner is taking her history. My friend tells her, "I have upper abdominal pain. My doctor found GI bleeding and anemia."

The nurse practitioner smiled patiently. "Now, dear, we don't know that." My friend had her family doctor's lab reports, but as often happens, the specialist accepted only reports from his own lab, "to eliminate error."

Before he would treat her, he required a gastroscopy, which is passing a scope down the throat and into the stomach to take a direct look. "We're pretty busy," the patient was told, "We can schedule you for six weeks from now." No medicine was supplied for the interim.

My friend returned to her family doctor, who gave her a precription for Prevacid. Taking that for six weeks healed her pain, and the gastroscope exam showed a stomach that by that time was almost normal.

Had she been my patient, I would have just given her the prescription at her first visit, and called the specialist only if she was not improving after a week. Tests for blood in the stool, for anemia, and for Helicobacter (a common cause of ulcer and bleeding) can be done in the office. A scope should still be done to rule out cancer, but the cancer will still be there when that specialist gets around to doing it.

My question to the specialist and his nurse would be, "Why *don't* you know that?" Why didn't you confirm or disprove the family doctor's data at first visit, at least look at his lab reports, and save the patient time, worry, and money?" Sometimes it seems like no one's listening to anyone else.

One more anecdote, because not paying attention really is a common fault:

Another friend of mine, call him "Joe", had bad lungs. Now, at age 75, he had been told there were cancer cells in his urine. In preparation for surgery in a couple of weeks at the regional hospital 45 miles away, Joe had had a consult with his lung doctor, and an EKG and blood work.

He is a worrier; he worried about what the the tests had found, and whether he would survive the anesthesia, the whole time he was waiting.

His wife called the hospital on the eve of surgery to verify the check-in time. "That surgery was cancelled," she was told. "there were no cancer cells in the last specimen."

No one had phoned to tell them. Joe now frets about all the time he spent worrying, and all the money he had paid for tests and consults.

I told him, "Look at the bright side, Joe. Think of all the money you're saving on the surgery you *don't* have to have."

But you'd think someone would have called him to let him know.

Chapter Ten:

Electronic Records

When everybody has computers, communication will be efficient. That's what medical experts say.

Yah. Just about everybody in medicine already *has* a computer. The trouble is, it can't communicate with all the other computer systems. Remember the 9/11 Commission report about New York's Twin Towers disaster? Firemen's radios weren't on the same wavelength as the police, and City Hall and the Port Authority had still different systems. Each system worked well individually, among its own customers. But when all systems needed to work together, there was chaos.

We're at that same stage with computers now. Recently a friend of mine had a tumor deep in his brain. He tells me that because the U of Washington medical center in Seattle uses a different computer system, the MRI pictures sent from his doctor's office in Spokane never arrived at the Seattle neurosurgeon's office. By the time his doctor was informed of the glitch and had Fed-Exed a duplicate MRI scan on a disk, treatment had been delayed by three weeks.

Doctor groups, hospitals, insurance carriers, and government offices are often in the same dilemma. Each listened to a different salesman, whose product was always "the best", and they spent hundreds of thousands of dollars buying, installing, training in the use of, and maintaining, their system, only to find out that the hospital or the next office down the road had a different system, and won't interface with theirs. They aren't about to pay out that amount of money again. "Let the other guy match up with me," is the common attitude.

The major intensive care center for central Washington State, at the time of this writing, has invested two million dollars establishing a universal computer system with its own doctors and several satellite centers in other cities in its area. But it doesn't interface with doctors or insurance agencies beyond that area. If you had surgery on your trip to Tennessee or Taiwan, better bring back your records on a disk.

The problem is further complicated by security issues needed to keep hackers from accessing patients' personal data.

Most computer networks have one or more backup systems. But in case of a region-wide shutdown caused by war, for example,[6] the backup systems could also shut down. In that case, only records on disc, printout, or microfilm would remain.

Sheer unabridged *volume* of electronic records can be a problem. A computer can transmit a patient's life-time record in a few seconds, but a human mind is needed at the receiving end to digest and act on it. Most doctors don't have time to read 200 pages of past visits; but are interested in the patient's basic problems over the years: what he's got, what has worked, and what has not.

Instead of letting the computer transmit the whole boring 200 pages when a patient moves to a new town, the sending doctor could summarize allergies, present medications, past illnesses, recent lab reports, etc. in a page or two. If the patient's new doctor needs further detail, an e-mail would usually be enough (or just ask the patient.) No nonsense about the computer automatically spitting out the whole summary again each time a progress note is added.

If the referring doctor gives a succinct hard copy or disk to the patient himself, the patient can carry it to wherever he chooses. Then it won't matter if two doctors' computers won't interface.

As for paperless prescriptions, they may be more legible than a doctor's writing, but they are no more free from other errors - spelling, wrong dosage, wrong drug, wrong patient, etc.

All of these and many other computer problems will eventually be solved. Among all the computer geeks in the world, someone will some day surely find a way to make all computer systems talk to each other. Computers are a valuable advance in medical information transfer, but so far they are not money savers. And mis-information is still spread—even more easily spread—by computer.

The solution to this portion of medical care cost is likely to take several years before a patient's record can be transferred electronically to everywhere in the USA, let alone to other locations.

CHAPTER ELEVEN:

POPULATION GROWTH

Some national resources are not infinite; among them are water, living space, fossil fuels, and forests. To which add money, (unless you believe that credit cards never come due.)

In the 1930s, the human world population was about two billion people. Now, only seventy-five years later, it is over six-and-a-half billion. It has tripled in seventy-five years.

For the United States, now at 307 million people, there is a birth every 7 seconds, a death every 13 seconds, a new international immigrant every 36 seconds, giving a net gain in population of one every ten seconds.[7] Six every minute of the year. 360 each hour; 8640 every day, three million per year, and accelerating.

Many things influence this rapid population growth: increasing life span, more effective treatment of disease, people's attitude toward ideal family size, to name only a few. But nowadays, seventy-two million more people are born than die in the world each year.[8] An average increase of 200,000 daily, despite wars, famines, epidemics, and other disasters.

Why should it matter? Can't the world produce enough food? It can, so far. Famine is more a problem of economics and distribution than of crop production. But population growth affects much more than just the food supply. Seventy-two million more people each year also need fuel, a place to live, schools, jobs, and medical care. Fresh water is becoming scarce in some parts of the world, and not only in desert regions.

Cities in southwestern United States and the adjacent part of Mexico have water demands that no longer are met by the Colorado River or aqueducts from more distant sources.[9]

I could go on about overcrowding and slums, migration of rural population to the cities, noise pollution, increasing crime, and increasing layers of bureaucrats needed to manage large nations. But the point is, population increase contributes to all these problems. Aside from real estate developers, manufacturers of baby products, and perhaps some politicians and army generals, I can't think of anyone who benefits from the world's chronic baby boom.

Lest some think this chapter is an argument for abortion, it is not. Abortion is a very poor way of population management, considering all the alternatives available (see below.)

But if we are to deal effectively with medical care costs—the real topic under focus here—we must deal with the birth rate. Calling it "playing God" is no more true for choosing to conceive, than it is for choosing to heal the sick. On the contrary, family planning is responsible stewardship.

The recent attention given to teen sexual abstinence is good, but it is only a small factor in world population growth, even when the program works. The major factor in the world's increasing population is the number of children that adult couples have. Many are not aware they have a choice. Actually, there have been a number of fairly inexpensive methods available for forty or more years now. Because they prevent conception rather than end a pregnancy, those of us who are anti-abortion should be glad that contraceptives decrease the number of pregnancies that people might otherwise choose to abort. Those who point out God's command to Adam and Eve to be fruitful and multiply might ponder whether the human race has not already done that. I am not aware of any command to have standing-room-only, or increasing urban sprawl.

Some want a large family. That's okay, if the parents can support their children emotionally and financially without going on public welfare. Most families are happier to have only two or three.[10]

Population increase, whether by more births or by immigration is not in itself helpful to lowering the cost of medical care. If we Americans, of whatever political, racial, or religious groups are serious about improving medical care and costs, for ourselves or the nation, the issue of family size must be considered. Choosing the number of children you want need not involve big philosophy discussions, planning commissions, or government funding. Most of the research on effectiveness and safety is already done, and there are many organizations ready and willing to give counsel and aid to those who wish it. But it does need a sense of personal responsibility in both men and women.

In my younger days, when my job description overseas included being medical consultant for my fellow volunteers, some would ask me for contraceptive advice—is there any effective natural method? I would answer, with tongue in cheek, "Orange juice."

That always got their interest. "Well, um, do you drink it before, or after?"

"Neither. You drink it instead."

It works, too, if the instructions were followed faithfully, but there are better ways to keep sperm and egg from uniting:

1) The rhythm method (some guesswork required) for those who can pinpoint the several days preceding and following ovulation, and can avoid sex during that period.
2) Condoms.
3) The vaginal diaphragm, if it fits well, and is inserted correctly, ahead of time, every time, and with appropriate cream or gel applied.
4) "Birth control" pills which prevent the ovary from releasing the egg. Most effective if started a couple of weeks in advance, and daily thereafter.

5) Birth control shots, taken once every three months, work the same way as the pill, but good memory is less a factor. For those who think being a few days late for the next shot doesn't matter, trust me, it does matter.

6) "Tying the tubes" for women, easiest done in the few days after childbirth, but a good GYN doctor can do it any time. I have seen rare cases of pregnancy after both tubes demonstrably were tied, but the method is effective in around 99% of cases.

7) Vasectomy for men. No, it does not make you fat or weak, and it can be done in the doctor's office in about a half-hour. Be sure you stay <u>at rest</u> for 24 hours afterward, and use condoms until the doctor checks your semen (4 - 6 weeks later) and pronounces it sperm-free. Men, your wife will appreciate you getting it done instead of her.

With this choice of methods available, the question of abortion should rarely arise. But the main point here is, with a lower birth rate, national resources, including medical care, become more manageable.

And the other part of the equation, reduction of the illegal immigration rate? That's beyond my field of experience. Except to observe that the country of Myanmar is an example that our legislators might consider. In Myanmar, being born in the country does not confer automatic citizenship, unless both parents can prove that *they* also were born in that country. That might at least lower the number of pregnant women crossing the border illegally to gain US citizenship for their child. Even if born here, the child would still have the same nationality as the parents, without automatic U.S. citizenship rights, unless he later went through the legal naturalization process.

Chapter Twelve:

Lowering the Cost of Care: Medical Insurance

Surfing TV on June 20th, 2009 I encountered George Will, the news columnist, speaking on C-Span saying the business of insurance companies is to provide health care. That is only partly true. It is what we expect to get for paying insurance premiums, yes. But actually, insurance companies' business goal is to make a profit; they pay doctors and hospitals to provide the care. But okay, their job is to make the system work, by cushioning the impact of sudden large medical costs, and most companies do that in most cases.

In an effort to keep their own costs manageable, they also set limits in the contract, intended to screen out overuse by the customer or overcharge by the doctor or hospital. Fair enough, if clearly understood in advance. They may limit your choice of doctors to those who have a working agreement with the company, but if that pool covers almost all the doctors in your area, and they allow exceptions when you have a medical emergency far from home, it can still work. They may require notification in advance of expected surgery, to rein in the occasional overly eager surgeon or the experimental treatment of unproven benefit.

But as new advances in medical treatment appear, requiring more skilled team members and new equipment, insurance companies feel the crunch and look for ways to cut their own costs further. If the claims are getting more frequent and more costly, one solution is to find some reason to not pay the claim.

"Appendicitis? But you didn't notify us before you signed the operation permit. Sorry."

"Nursing home care? You were in the hospital two days, and we cover nursing home care only if you were in the hospital at least three days prior to transfer."

"Physiotherapy? Your employer's new contract with us this year doesn't cover that." And so on.

What comes out of all this is, single families and small groups are more risky to insure than very large groups. Profits from a pool of only one thousand members are wiped out if one of them needs a liver transplant. But if you are the one needing a liver transplant and your claim is rejected, your life is what's wiped out. And if the small insurer has to cover several organ transplants and raises the premium rate high enough to pay for them, your new insurance rate could bankrupt your family or your employer. That has happened.

Some argue, "Let insurance companies work it out. Keep government out of it." But the insurance companies have not been able to work it out, and the government is the only one so far with enough clout to blow the whistle on all those who try to game the system—some of the doctors, some of the lawyers, some in the pharmaceutical industry, some of the insurers, some of the patients, some business enterprises, some in Congress, all lobbying for their own agendas. Congress is at least answerable to the people every two years.

Most of the prospering nations have some type of single-payer health care system. I don't have the financial knowledge to say whether it's best run by government directly, or by a non-profit group answerable to the government we elect. But it's too easy for a for-profit insurance business to siphon off bigger dividends for the share holders, or bonuses for the executives at the expense of their real customers, the insured. So far they have been unable, or unwilling, to address this problem. Many legitimate claims are denied, and millions have no insurance at all. Any treatment the uninsured get is ultimately paid by us taxpayers, either in higher taxes or higher premiums, while the insurance companies keep their profits.

In my opinion, the larger the pool of insured, the lower the overall cost of American medical care. That's if the managers of the pool are competent and answerable to the American public, either through Congress or through some designated group with power to make sure that the insured have recourse. It's not a matter of socialized medicine versus total laissez-faire. Medicare and Medicaid are already socialized medicine run by the government, but few want to give up the benefits they provide. They are not perfect programs, but they are better than what the senior citizens and the poor had before.

The public and the medical profession agree on at least one point: A third-echelon insurance clerk—with neither the training to be familiar with the medical problem, nor the perspective to know the individual patient's needs—should not be making the decisions to accept or reject a claim.

A hundred competitive for-profit insurance companies are not the answer. Faced with a life-threatening crisis, the ill patient with a denied claim has neither the time nor the stamina to go searching for another company, or fight the denial in court. And physicians, confronted with such denials almost every day, can't spend their time defending a diagnosis or treatment to someone who hasn't any background to go by except a company rule book.

In my opinion, a single-payer system, answerable to the people or their representatives in Congress, is the best way to go. And if not that, at least a government-run plan should be one option for the citizen to choose from, especially in regions where few competitive choices are available. The main point is, there must be affordable insurance choices for all citizens.

Chapter Thirteen:

The Patient's Role

The patient can help lower costs too. All the medical advice in the world will be useless if the patient is not motivated to listen or act.

The doctor can counsel an obese patient on diet and exercise, but only the patient has control over the amount of food consumed, or the self-discipline to exercise regularly and effectively.

There are effective medicines for high blood pressure and for diabetes, and the patient can learn to self-check blood pressure and blood sugar quite easily, with only occasional visits to the doctor. But the medicine does no good on the shelf.

Vaccines are effective for prevention of a number of severe diseases, but it's the parent's responsibility to see that the child gets them. Some parents don't want to take the small risk of adverse effect from the vaccine itself. But I have personally witnessed non-immunized children die from tetanus, whooping cough, diphtheria, or measles, and trust me, you don't want to risk that for your child.

When a Family Member is Sick, Do Your Homework First. You will save time in the doctor's office, get more effective treatment, or sometimes can avoid the trip altogether.

Observe the sick one's behavior and symptoms, so you can give a brief summary to the doctor or his nurse. They will usually want to know if he has a fever. It's no help for you to say, "Well, he doesn't feel hot." Take his temperature; a clinical thermometer is a good household investment. How is he breathing? What does he look like? Sweating? Pale? Does he have vomiting or diarrhea? Pain?

Be ready to tell the doctor the name and the dose of each medicine being taken. "It's a little white pill" is not helpful. Adults who take a whole lot of stuff should carry an up-to-date list on their person, just as they do with a driver's license or medical ID. If possible, bring the whole set of medicine bottles along, unless they require a bucket, in which case a list will do.

Some things are reasonably safe to watch for a while. Many colds, low-grade fevers, or general aches are caused by virus infections which will be better in a day or two. But if you are worried, phone your doctor, or whoever is taking his calls.

Save the hospital emergency room for real emergencies. I know, they are required to treat you if you show up at their door, but you are held responsible for paying their bill, and it's likely to be five or ten times what you would be charged at a doctor's office. A bad injury, or a severe illness, is reason to go to the ER, but don't be a "frequent flyer."

Not only could the nation's medical costs be billions of dollars cheaper by everyone following these common sense bits of advice, but your own savings could be many dollars.

Your life-style and general attitude affect your health, too. Chronic anger, self-centeredness, lack of life purpose, addiction—be it drugs, porn, gambling, eating, watching TV, or whatever—all influence your physical health. Brain and body are physically connected, and what occupies your mind influences your blood pressure, tension, sleep or lack thereof, and general well-being.

Medicines, when properly used, can have dramatic effects; but more pills are not necessarily the path to recovery. Sometimes taking time to step back and assess your life and goals is of even greater benefit than reliance on pain pills and tranquilizers.

And less expensive, too, both nationally and personally.

Chapter Fourteen:

Watchdogs and "Government Interference"

Think about this a minute. You maybe have a burglar alarm at your business site, or a watchdog at your home. Military installations routinely post sentries. And most of us are familiar with airport security inspections. None of these guardians are violating Constitutional rights. You may not like the inconvenience, but few would dispute the need. That's because there are occasional people out there, whether citizens or aliens is irrelevant, who do not respect your property or life.

So why is a watchdog agency such as the Federal Aviation Authority, or the Federal Drug Administration, or the Securities and Exchange Commission, or any of dozens of other government groups considered "interfering" when they blow a whistle on the shenanigans of Wall Street, or lax safety inspection, or executive greed?

Someone does need to blow a whistle when a smelter lets clouds of lead dust billow out of the smokestack unfiltered. Or when a drunk takes the wheel of a car. Or when a bank or insurance company risks its customers' investments by loaning billions of dollars to high risk enterprises.

When an industry persuades Congress that deregulation of pharmaceuticals, or neglecting building codes, or cutting taxes are in the public interest, there is often a thin line between good business practices and corruption.

When a physician, called about a patient, doesn't see the patient but orders some medicine over the phone, and then charges the patient's insurance a fee for doing an exam, "because he is taking the responsibility," he's getting pretty close to fraud. That's a nasty word, but sometimes it has to be said, and it is another large factor in the rising cost of medical care.

There are trade-offs. If the government is to repair highways, it must find funds to pay for the workers, the material, and the equipment. If there is obvious waste in a program, it doesn't make sense to let the money continue to bleed away while the work stands idle. Nor does it make sense to continue to borrow endlessly and let hundreds of billions of dollars go to pay interest on the debt. And it doesn't make sense for a First World nation to leave 15% of its citizens medically uninsured. This makes the taxpayer or those with insurance pay the cost for the uninsured.

What Government Could Do Better: One of the tasks of Congress is to create laws for public benefit. To leave no doubt of what the law means, Congress adds regulatory clauses, often to the extent of a thousand pages or more. That length creates a lot of doubts of its own. For one thing, I doubt that many lawmakers, or their aides, have read the whole thousand pages carefully enough to grasp their full meaning.

How about a two or three-page summary stating *concisely* the purpose and actions required by the act, to which the other 997 pages must conform? And if any don't conform, they must be revised until they do. Keep the focus on the intended final result or goal.

Easing the Doctor Shortage: Is there a shortage of doctors in the USA? Depends on how you use them. In the 1990s I could get along with one office receptionist/typist/billing clerk and one nurse/lab tech; that's two full-time workers. There weren't nearly as many government forms to fill out then, compared with now. Recently, TV Evening News featured medicine in Massachusetts, where medical insurance for everyone has already been in effect since July, 2007. One family practice doctor said it now took eleven clerks to handle the paperwork. She herself could handle only 3,000 patient visits per year [at 200 to 250 working days/year = 12 to 15 patients per day. The average used to be around 20 to 24.] The Evening News made the point that even though 97% of Massachusetts people now have insurance, they have difficulty getting an appointment. Not enough doctors.

I remember Massachusetts in the news about fifteen years ago, too. At that time, many of the state's baby doctors were moving to other states because they could not afford the escalating costs of malpractice insurance in Mass. I suppose some of the family doctors who also delivered babies left for the same reason. Massachusetts appears to be a good case study of how malpractice rates and paper work can limit the number of doctors and/or the amount of time available to see patients. The government—both Congress and Health and Human Services—should act to clear those log jams.

The public wants action to produce a medical care act that reduces waste, increases efficiency, and addresses the problems of 45 million uninsured citizens. Instead, both houses of Congress, and many agencies besides, spend time and effort jockeying for political power rather than addressing the merits and flaws of the act they are trying to put together. Such delays cost money. Catch phrases and frank misstatement of meaning, endlessly put before the public in TV ads and talk shows, don't get the job done.

Congress cannot expect to mandate new standards of care without funding them. It is hypocrisy to say "no new taxes," while cutting federal funding, leaving the states to finance the new federal law through new state taxes.

Chapter Fifteen:

Other Important Players in Reducing Medical Costs

The Nurses: Hospitals are closing some units, even some badly needed emergency rooms, because they lack funds to keep them open. But while present job lay-offs will ease as the economy improves, the 50% of nurses who are nearing retirement keep on growing older even during lay-off periods, and fewer of them will be available several years from now.

The bottleneck in nurse recruitment, nurses tell me, is not a lack of students, but the lack of nursing instructors to teach them. Apparently, not enough nurses are taking teaching jobs that pay only half of what they deservedly earn in their present jobs. This is a crisis that needs fixing very soon.

Nurses, what's the answer? I know you are vocal in the nursing journals, but I don't hear your voices much in the general public debate. Is this going to require government grants that go mostly for more commissions to study the problem, or is there some common sense solution?

Nurse Practitioners can often help augment family practice doctors, but with the present shortage of nursing school faculty, increasing their numbers may be as hard as increasing primary care doctors.

The Lawyers: Lawsuits are one of a doctor's greatest fears. That can be good or bad. Good, because the doctor will take care to avoid errors. Bad, because a patient may sue him anyway, and because the extra tests and consultations he orders to prevent lawsuits add considerably to the cost of care, even though of little benefit to the patient. Even if the doctor wins, the publicity has harmed his reputation, and his malpractice insurance premiums go up.

The State of Idaho, and I suppose some other states but not all, have an independent pre-trial panel to screen out cases deemed "without merit". The panel includes an attorney, a physician, and a lay person, who examine the records, take testimony, and give a non-binding opinion. The plaintiff may choose to proceed with trial despite an unfavorable recommendation, but pre-screening gives both plaintiff and defendant a sense of whether the case justifies a long and expensive trial, and it decreases the court's caseload and costs.

News Media: News publications and TV can be important sources of facts about medical care. But facts are rarely enough to fill 24 hours, even with commercial breaks. Editorializing and emoting often skew facts to favor a predetermined agenda. During recent debates on medical care, the talking heads on TV seem more intent on drowning each other out than bringing information before the public that might be useful in reducing costs.

The Emergency Room: ER doctors are in a bind. They are required by law to treat anyone with a medical emergency, but many non-emergency patients use the ER because they have no place else to go, and it takes the ER nurses and doctors time to tell the difference. Even in small town ERs, the load can be overwhelming. Add to it drug addicts, traffic accidents, domestic abuse victims, and just plain lonely people. You don't want to miss a heart attack, a bleeding brain, a surgical abdomen, a potential suicide, so any of these and hundreds of other conditions require blood tests, CT scans, EKGs and/or observation, to diagnose them properly.

A doctor who has seen and known the patient for years would sort out the case more quickly and accurately, with fewer tests and lower costs. In an ER where the patient is a stranger, all the work must be done from scratch. Even if you wake the patient's own doctor at 2 a.m., the first thing he's going to ask is, what have you found out so far?

So it goes back to a previous chapter: with insurance, many people could avoid the ER and go to a doctor who knows them, and who will have some hope of being paid for his work, even if it's less than he would like to charge. Medicare does this for senior citizens; Medicaid does it for the extremely poor. Now we need to see to the needs of the low income worker and family, where a $175 first visit fee, or even a $30 fee for each of three kids for a 5-minute school sports physical is out of reach. (What ever happened to the doctors who set aside a morning once a year to do those school physicals free?)

Doctors, a good many people are looking at you at this point. No one realistically expects a return to the six-dollar office visit, but if the country can bring about some legal reform, at the same time that you are curbing the impulse to overtest and overtreat, could your charges climb at a slower rate, instead of three times as fast as inflation?

Chapter Sixteen:

Where Do We Go From Here?

The President and Congress are already working to make medical care more affordable and more effective. This is not easy, because even as they work, researchers are discovering new treatments or tests for more diseases for our growing population. All of which tends to further increase the nation's future medical costs. At the same time, many citizens are expressing fears that they will be left out, rationed, get higher taxes, or get no personal choices.

And at the same time, lobbyists are calling attention to the special concerns of their clients—doctors, lawyers, educators, nurses, hospitals, unions, senior citizens, pharmaceutical industry, insurance industry, conservatives, liberals, and so on—anyone who stands to gain or lose, depending on the outcome. Whether individual members of Congress will be able to solve the needs of the whole nation, and fund that solution in a way acceptable to their constituents back home, we can only hope and pray.

Finding a solution to a major crisis (in this case the explosion of medical care costs) is not an election campaign, nor a shouting match to assign blame, but a calm and reasoned search for action that will benefit everyone as much as is humanly possible. Many members of both parties in the Senate and House more of them than when the debate started—are seriously seeking some way that will work.

"Pick the lower fruit first" It makes sense to focus first on what can reduce large existing costs more quickly, and without requiring new commissions or agencies. One aim of medical reform, after all, is to lessen government costs where possible, rather than increase them by buying everything in the store.

In my opinion, early cost reductions will most likely come from two sources:

(1) increased use of **competitive generic medicines**, reserving the newer drugs for when no substitute exists, and not merely using the new drug because it is widely advertised on TV. The public interest is served when government programs like Medicare, Medicaid, VA, and other large contractors are allowed to seek competitive bids from their suppliers. But a switch to generics will not be enough to lower the costs, if competitive bidding is banned.

Allow citizens to fill their prescriptions abroad, provided the medicine is manufactured in a country with manufacturing standards enforced and inspected by a competent agency. My experience abroad suggests that that would include most "First World" nations and a good number of "emerging" nations. There are indeed foreign sources of medicines in some Third World countries that are not trustworthy, but many other countries have standards as high as USA—patterned on the USA's Federal Drug Administration standards in many cases.

(2) **Encourage States to cap non-economic damages in lawsuits.** This has worked in Texas, California,

and Nevada. It will rapidly relieve malpractice insurance costs, will attract more new doctors to the state, and will encourage doctors to get out of the habit of overtesting and overtreating, thus lowering patient costs still more. One of the current Senate plans having some bipartisan support proposes a Public Health Trust Fund to fund bonuses to states for instituting medical malpractice reform. I would prefer that states do that on their own, without need for bonuses, but if that's what it takes to prime the pump for cost reduction, so be it.

Notice that compensation for actual damages will still be fully allowed; penalties for malpractice will still be awarded, and doctors (and other defendants) will still need some malpractice insurance; but unrealistically large awards will be regulated.

The argument that the elderly will recover only a small compensation because they have no future earnings is nonsense: $250,000 (or $500,000 if the state so decides) plus damages, is more than the average senior citizen has in the bank, even after the attorney takes his 30%.

Some other remedies—making electronic records systems communicate with each other, for instance, or funding an insurance system that will include all citizens at an acceptable cost are excellent objectives, but will take more time.

Start individually with the ones that are already seen to work. Take it not too fast—better to have solid results than no results at all. Just as Medicare has had to be adjusted sometimes, this present medical plan will also need re-examination and adjustment as problems become apparent. No bill is perfect from the start.

(3) Stricter oversight on government regulating agencies. Try not to create more agencies— that's what costs

big bucks. FDA, CDC, state boards of medicine, etc., are already in place. Encourage them to do the jobs they were created to do, stopping the fraud, the free-loading, the over-use, and abuse of the system.

CHAPTER SEVENTEEN:
WORKING TOGETHER

Don't despair just yet, if your job is gone. As the economy begins to recover, as it gives signs of doing, there will be need for new construction, new products and new services, which means more jobs eventually.

But as employers trim costs to survive, that will translate temporarily into fewer employees to do the same amount of work (when remaining workers are reassigned, and more labor saving equipment is brought into use.) The downside of cutting costs is that those costs often represented jobs.

Most money is spent, in the end, to pay those who produce goods and services. Even the cost of a new power plant or factory is mostly paying the workers—those that work on site plus those who produce the materials shipped in. And beyond that, the food, housing, fuel, education, and medical care to supply all these workers creates still more jobs, in a widening circle.

Meanwhile, there will be questions, there will be complaints, there will be some errors. We live in a democracy, and it's proper for anybody to comment. We also live in a civilized, God-fearing society, and it's proper to comment without dissing an opponent in either word or tone.

The problems of American medical care are not easily solved, but they will surely get even worse, as costs keep going up, if we do nothing but debate. We need to work together, in spite of political differences, to get a viable medical care plan now, not two years from now, not four years from now. This project will affect all of us, and our children, and our grandchildren.

Notes

1 One daughter works in cardiac electrophysiology in a regional hospital, and is on the board of directors of a rural hospital. Another daughter is a retired army surgical nurse, now civilian nurse manager of a military hospital's operating rooms. The youngest daughter is nurse-manager of the critical care unit in a regional medical center in a nearby state. My wife, after years as an office nurse, is now a volunteer in the local Hospice program.

2 The reader can find many sources for cost information by Googling Consumer Health Ratings, Emergency Room, typical average cost. I surveyed reports from Florida, Minnesota, and Vermont, plus an additional survey by G.M.P. Employers Retiree Trust.

3 Acute Cardiac Life Support and Acute Trauma Life Support certificates are required retraining courses every 2-4 years, in most emergency rooms.

4 The state of Oregon has experimented with making immunizations and other basic care available to all, at the cost of having to deny public payment for some costly treatments (bone marrow transplants, for example.)

5 Ashley Hawkins III, Washington Post, quoted in the Spokane, WA Spokesman-Review June 21, 2009, page A4

6 Cyber attack blocks federal Web sites; Associated Press report, in Spokane Spokesman-Review Jul 8, 2009, page A3.

7 Source: United Nations, *World Population Prospects, The 1998 Revision*; and estimates by the Population Reference Bureau.

8 ibid.

9   Tearfund, a British organization, points out the shrinkage in Africa's large Lake Chad to only 5% of its 1967 size. And a 53-foot drop in the level of Asia's Aral Sea, once the world's fourth biggest inland sea, has almost wiped it out.

10   The desire for small families is not just a western cultural trait. When I practiced medicine in rural Thailand, I asked every woman patient between ages 15 and 45 during one twelve-month period, "How many children have you had? How many are still living? And how many more children do you want?"

Women nearing the end of childbearing (age 40 to 45) in 1966-67, in that part of Thailand, had had an average of eight children. The town dwellers had seen an average of two of them die; the hill village dwellers had lost an average of four. When asked how many more they wanted, most with more than two living children said they wanted no more. (Parents with children of all one sex sometimes wanted to try one more time.) Most with two or more children asked for contraceptive help on their own initiative, and by 1981 we had about 1,200 women coming every three months for contraception. (The most popular method at that time was a shot of DMPA, trade name Depo Provera, every three months.)

This surprised me, because most of them were low-income farmers with no social security plan, and the popular belief among western sociologists of that time was that the desire to limit number of children comes only after a rise in the standard of living. But in a rural town with few telephones, few newspaper readers, few television sets, and no advertising campaign (except a small sign announcing availability of family planning help) some villages hired buses every three months to bring their women in for their shot. Family planning clinics reduced the annual population increase rate in Thailand from 3½% to 2% between 1963 and 1983. The techniques, safety, and side effects of popular family planning methods are well studied.